Caterpillar to Butterfly

Laura Marsh

NATIONAL GEOGRAPHIC

Washington, D.C.

For Owen and Mason,
who are evolving every day before me
—L. F. M.

Design by YAY! Design

Paperback ISBN: 978-1-4263-0920-5   Library ISBN: 978-1-4263-0921-2

Photo credits

Cover, Ralph A Clevenger/Photolibrary; 1, James Urbach/SuperStock; 2, FotoVeto/Shutterstock; 4 (top), George D. Lepp/Corbis; 4 (bottom), Christian Musat/Shutterstock; 5, Le Do/Shutterstock; 6 (left), ethylalkohol/Shutterstock; 6 (right), fotohunter/Shutterstock; 7 (top left), First Light/Getty Images; 7 (bottom left), Ingram; 7 (top right), ArtisticPhoto/Shutterstock; 7 (bottom right), Jens Stolt/Shutterstock; 8 (top), M. Williams Woodbridge/National Geographic Stock; 8 (bottom), Carolyn Pepper/National Geographic My Shot ; 9 (top), Steve Irvine/National Geographic My Shot; 9 (bottom), Cathy Keifer/Shutterstock; 10, Darren5907/Alamy; 11 (top), Alex Wild/Visuals Unlimited/Corbis; 11 (top center), Michael & Patricia Fogden/Corbis; 11 (bottom center), Danita Delimont/Getty Images; 11 (bottom), Ingo Arndt/Foto Natura/Minden Pictures/National Geographic Stock; 12, Papilio/Alamy; 13, Gerry Ellis/Minden Pictures/National Geographic Stock; 14, Nigel Cattlin/Visuals Unlimited/Corbis; 16, Cathy Keifer/iStockphoto.com; 18, M. Williams Woodbridge/National Geographic Stock; 19, M. Williams Woodbridge/National Geographic Stock; 20, Awei/Shutterstock; 22 (top), Murugesan Anbazhagan/National Geographic My Shot; 22 (center), Robert Shantz/Alamy; 22 (bottom), WitR/Shutterstock; 23 (top), Jaime Wykle/National Geographic My Shot; 23 (center), James Laurie/Shutterstock; 23 (bottom), The Natural History Museum/Alamy; 24 (top), Christian Meyn/National Geographic My Shot; 24 (bottom), Charles Melton/Visuals Unlimited; 25, Gary Meszaros/Visuals Unlimited; 26, gracious_tiger/Shutterstock; 27, Hans Christoph Kappel/naturepl.com; 28, Gay Bumgarner/Alamy; 29, Alivepix/Shutterstock; 30 (left), Robert Pickett/Corbis; 30 (right), April Moore/National Geographic My Shot; 31(top left), TessarTheTegu/Shutterstock; 31 (bottom left), David Plummer/Alamy; 31 (top right), Konstantnin/Shutterstock; 31 (bottom right), Renant Cheng/National Geographic Stock; 32 (top left), Christian Meyn/National Geographic My Shot; 32 (bottom left), Joe Petersburger/National Geographic Stock; 32 (top right), nodff/Shutterstock; 32 (bottom right), Cathy Keifer/iStockphoto.com; header throughout, NuConcept/Shutterstock.

Printed in the United States of America

12/WOR/1

To learn the names of butterflies, caterpillars, or moths not labeled in the book, see page 32.

Table of Contents

Riddle

What starts as an egg,

then walks on many legs,

and then
uses wings
to fly?

A butterfly!

Beautiful Butterflies

Butterflies are fun to watch. They fly with loops and dives. Some have bright colors. Some have bold patterns, too.

Four Stages

It's also fun to watch butterflies change. They change a lot in their short lives. In fact, there are four stages in a butterfly's life:

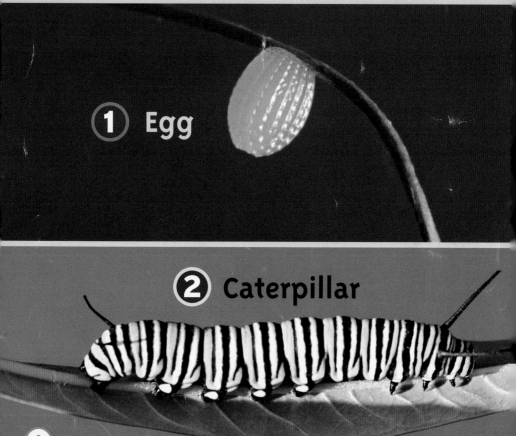

1 Egg

2 Caterpillar

3 Chrysalis

Say *KRISS-ah-liss*

4 Butterfly

Monarch butterfly

Catch Word

STAGES: Steps of how something grows

9

Stage **1** Egg

A mother butterfly lays many eggs on a leaf or branch. Each egg is close to food (caterpillar food, that is).

Malayan egg-fly butterfly

Butterfly eggs come in all different shapes.

Stage **2** Caterpillar

The tiny caterpillar bites a hole in the egg. It crawls out. The caterpillar is very hungry.

The caterpillar eats its shell. Then it eats the leaf it's on. The caterpillar moves to another leaf. It eats that, too.

The caterpillar grows and grows. It gets too big for its skin. It sheds its old skin like a snake.

Small white butterfly caterpillar

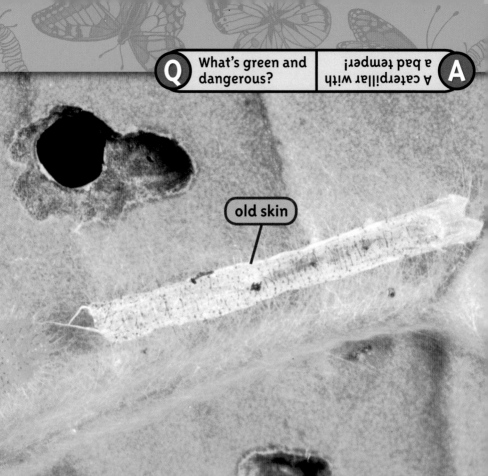

old skin

The new skin fits for a while. But then the caterpillar is too big for that skin, too. Caterpillars shed their skin four or five times.

Monarch butterfly caterpillar

Stage **3** Chrysalis

By now the caterpillar is ready to rest. It hangs upside down. It sheds its skin one more time.

stages of a caterpillar forming its chrysalis

The new layer is called a chrysalis. It is a hard shell. Inside the caterpillar is changing. It stays in the chrysalis for ten to fourteen days.

Butterfly

The chrysalis moves. It splits open. The butterfly wiggles out. Its wings are wet and crumpled.

Julia butterfly

Blood pumps into the butterfly's wings. They get bigger and harden. The wings dry. Now the butterfly is ready to fly.

Have a good trip, butterfly!

Time for lunch!

A butterfly doesn't eat plants like a caterpillar. It has no mouth.

A butterfly drinks nectar from flowers. It drinks juice from fruit. A tube on its head works like a straw.

Slurrrp!

Catch Word

NECTAR: A sugary liquid found in flowers

Cool Butterfly Facts

1

The world's smallest butterfly is the blue pygmy. It's the length of a pushpin from wing to wing.

2

Butterfly wings are covered with tiny scales.

3

Butterflies are found all over the world, except in Antarctica and the driest deserts.

4

There are about 17,000 kinds of butterflies in the world.

5

Butterflies taste with their feet! They have taste sensors there.

6

The world's largest butterfly is the Queen Alexandra birdwing. It's as long as a ruler from wing to wing.

Back off!

Caterpillars and butterflies are a tasty snack for predators. But they have tricks to keep predators away.

Some hide using camouflage.

Some can be deadly to eat.

Some look like other things.

Moth or Butterfly?

Butterfly

antennae are thin and have little knobs at end

bodies are slender

can be brightly colored

mostly fly during the day

Say an-TEN-ay

Moths and butterflies look alike. Here's how you can tell them apart.

Moth

antennae slim to a point and look like feathers

bodies are fat and furry

usually brown, tan, or white

mostly fly at night

27

Bring Butterflies to You

You can bring butterflies to your backyard. Make a butterfly garden! But first ask an adult for help.

Swallowtail butterfly

Here's what you'll need:

✓ plants that are local to your area

✓ plants that bloom at different times

✓ orange, purple, yellow, pink, and red flowers

✓ flowers that are clustered together

✓ flat-topped flowers

✓ a sunny spot for butterflies to rest, like a flat stone

✓ a wet or watery spot for butterflies to drink

✓ no chemicals (which can kill butterflies and caterpillars)

What in the World?

These pictures show close-up views of butterfly things. Use the hints below to figure out what's in the pictures. Answers on page 31.

HINT: A caterpillar starts here.

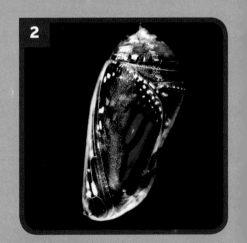

HINT: Big changes happen inside.

3

HINT: It's an all-day eater!

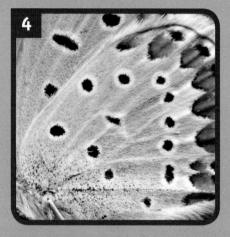

4

HINT: This is covered with scales.

5

HINT: It uses this to hide from predators.

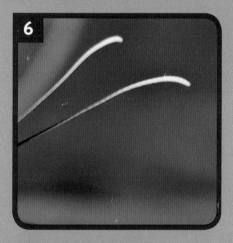

6

HINT: You won't find these on your head!

Answers: 1. egg, 2. chrysalis, 3. caterpillar, 4. butterfly wing, 5. camouflage, 6. antennae

CAMOUFLAGE: An animal's natural color or shape that helps it hide from an enemy

NECTAR: A sugary fluid found in flowers

PREDATOR: An animal that eats other animals

STAGES: Steps of how something grows

Additional butterfly species names: Page 6, Left to right: Blue morpho butterfly, Blue African swallowtail; Page 7, Top to bottom: Panacea prola butterfly, Bog copper butterfly, Old World swallowtail, Apollo butterfly; Page 12, Cabbage white butterfly caterpillar; Page 13, Crimson-patched longwing caterpillar; Page 24, Top to bottom: Cracker butterfly, Pipevine swallowtail caterpillar; Page 25, Spicebush swallowtail caterpillar; Page 26, Cairns birdwing butterfly; Page 27, Emperor moth.